Dirty Denis

VIKING KESTREL

Published by the Penguin Group
Viking Penguin Inc., 40 West 23rd Street, New York, New York 10010, U.S.A.
27 Wrights Lane, London W8 5TZ, England
Penguin Books Australia Ltd, Ringwood, Victoria, Australia
Penguin Books Canada Ltd, 2801 John Street, Markham, Ontario, Canada L3R 1B4
Penguin Books (N.Z.) Ltd, 182–190 Wairau Road, Auckland 10, New Zealand

Penguin Books Ltd, Registered Offices: Harmondsworth, Middlesex, England

First published in Great Britain 1988 by
Hamish Hamilton Children's Books
First American edition published in 1989
Published simultaneously in Canada
1 3 5 7 9 10 8 6 4 2
Text copyright © 1988 by Sally Grindley
Illustrations copyright © 1988 by Paul Dowling

ISBN 0–670–82686–3

Printed in West Germany

Dirty Denis

SALLY GRINDLEY

ILLUSTRATED BY PAUL DOWLING

Viking Kestrel

Dirty Denis never washed and never brushed his teeth.
"If you don't brush your teeth," said his mother, "they'll all drop out."

Dirty Denis's room was always a mess, and his schoolwork was always covered with dirty fingerprints.

"If you don't tidy up your room," said his dad, "I'll do it for you and throw everything away."

"I can't read your work," said his teacher "You'll end up at the bottom of the class."

But Dirty Denis didn't have time to worry about being clean and neat. There were too many other things to do. A lick with a wash cloth and a flick with a toothbrush was the most he ever managed.

So dirty Dirty Denis was and dirty Dirty Denis stayed.

Dirty though Dirty Denis was, his mother loved him, his dad loved him, and even his teachers liked him. "He'll grow out of it some day," they said.

And dirty though Dirty Denis was, he was the most popular boy in his school. "Energetic, friendly and generous," said his school report.

Then one day Dirty Denis met Neat Nora.
She was neat from the top of her not-a-
hair-out-of-place-head to the tips of her
never-a-scuff shoes.

Not many of the children liked Neat
Nora.

Dirty Denis was fascinated by her.

Neat Nora didn't like him.
"How can you like him?" she said to
anyone who would listen. "He's dirty."

"Why do you worry about her?" said Dirty Denis's friends. "She's always nasty to you. Just because she's neat she thinks she's better than anyone else."

But Dirty Denis didn't listen.

He watched her in the playground at recess.

She stuck her neat tongue out at him.

He sat near her at lunch. She turned her neat back on him.

He waited for her outside school. She minced neatly past and snickered at him.

For days he did nothing but think about her. He ignored all his friends.

In the evenings he sat in his bedroom and stared at the walls.

He got into trouble with his teacher
because he didn't pay attention in class.

Then one morning a different Denis walked into school. His face and ears were scrubbed pink, his fingernails were polished white, his hair was plastered down and his black shoes gleamed.

That same morning Neat Nora drew a portrait of him in the school hall.

No brains
Dirty Denis

Beetles →

Spiders ←

Ugly face →

dirty
sticky
out
ears ←

Last
years
breakfast →

→ Yellow
teeth

filthy
old
Jumper. →

last
weeks
sandwich ←

Broken
mirror
that
he
looked in.

HORRIBLE
STINK

mouse by
killed
smelly feet. ↙

Dirty Denis felt terrible. He stood in the playground at recess and stared at his shiny shoes.

He stood in the playground at lunch and stared at his clean fingernails.

His friends watched and wondered what to do. "That was a dirty trick to play," they agreed. "Let's go and cheer him up."

They went over to where Denis stood, and laughed and joked and teased him about the way he looked.

Dirty Denis smiled.

They asked him to play ball with them.

Dirty Denis said yes.

He ran and ran. His hair got untidy, his
hands got grubby, his shoes got muddy,
but as he ran he began to enjoy himself
for the first time in weeks.

As he ran he began to forget about Neat Nora and her dirty trick.

When he went home his mom and dad
were delighted to see him looking
cheerful again. His teacher was delighted
to have him paying attention again.

His friends were all delighted to have him
back in their gang again.

As for Neat Nora, they took no notice of
her. Nor did Dirty Denis from then on.

And one day Dirty Denis grew out of his dirty, scruffy ways and became just . . . Denis.